LIFE LESSONS FROM BATHSHEBA

Study by Susan M. Pigott
Commentary by Tony W. Cartledge

Free downloadable Teaching Guide for this study available at

NextSunday.com/teachingguides

NextSunday Resources
6316 Peake Road
Macon, Georgia 31210-3960
1-800-747-3016
©2012 by NextSunday Resources
All rights reserved.
Printed in the United States of America.

Library of Congress Cataloging-in-Publication Data

CIP Information on file.

TABLE OF CONTENTS

Life Lessons from Bathsheba

HOW TO USE THIS STUDY

NextSunday Resources Adult Bible Studies are designed to help adults study Scripture seriously within the context of the larger Christian tradition and, through that process, find their faith renewed, challenged, and strengthened. We study the Scriptures because we believe they affect our current lives in important ways. Each study contains the following three components:

Study Guide

Each study guide lesson is arranged in four movements:

Reflecting recalls a contemporary story, anecdote, example, or illustration to help us anticipate the session's relevance in our lives.

Studying is centered on giving the biblical material in-depth attention while often surrounding it with helpful insights from theology, ethics, church history, and other areas.

Understanding helps us find relevant connections between our lives and the biblical message.

What About Me? provides brief statements that help unite life issues with the meaning of the biblical text.

Commentary

Each study guide lesson is accompanied by an additional, in-depth commentary on the biblical material. Written by a different author than the study guide, each commentary gives the opportunity for learners to approach the Scripture text from a separate but complementary viewpointt.

Teaching Guide

In addition to the provided study guide and commentary, *NextSunday Resources* also provides a *free* downloadable teaching guide, available at NextSunday.com. Each teaching guide gives the teacher tools for focusing on the content of each study guide lesson through additional commentary and Bible background information. Through teacher helps and teaching options, each teaching guide also provides substance for variety and choice in the preparation of each lesson.

NextSunday
Resources

STUDY INTRODUCTION

Who was Bathsheba? We know her primarily as the woman with whom David committed adultery. But the biblical text tells us much more. Bathsheba was the daughter of Eliam, the widow of Uriah, the wife of David, and the grieving mother of a seven-day-old baby who died tragically. She later gave birth to Solomon and played an instrumental role in claiming and securing the throne on her son's behalf.

In this series of lessons, we will observe her transformation. The first lesson, "The Adultress?" considers the familiar story of David and Bathsheba, but it poses the question, "Was Bathsheba a willing participant or an unwitting victim of David's sexual desire?" In the second lesson, we discover that Bathsheba's child is sick and dying, a tiny victim of David's sin. We grieve with Bathsheba and ask "Why?" with her, trying to find comfort, as she did, in the birth of her second baby, Solomon. By the third lesson, Solomon is a grown man. When his brother Adonijah claims the throne, Solomon does not fight for the kingship—Bathsheba does! Finally, in the last lesson, Bathsheba is instrumental in the demise of Adonijah, thereby ensuring that Solomon's throne is no longer contested.

Who was Bathsheba? She was a complex figure who developed from the silent object of David's lust into a powerful, vocal, and influential queen mother.

1

THE ADULTRESS?

2 Samuel 11:2-5, 26-27a

Central Question

What can I do in a no-win situation?

Scripture

2 Samuel 11:2-5; 26-27a 2 It happened, late one afternoon, when David rose from his couch and was walking about on the roof of the king's house, that he saw from the roof a woman bathing; the woman was very beautiful. 3 David sent someone to inquire about the woman. It was reported, "This is Bathsheba daughter of Eliam, the wife of Uriah the Hittite." 4 So David sent messengers to get her, and she came to him, and he lay with her. (Now she was purifying herself after her period.) Then she returned to her house. 5 The woman conceived; and she sent and told David, "I am pregnant".... 26 When the wife of Uriah heard that her husband was dead, she made lamentation for him. 27a When the mourning was over, David sent and brought her to his house, and she became his wife, and bore him a son. But the thing that David had done displeased the Lord.

Reflecting

In the movie *Sophie's Choice* (Universal Pictures, 1982), the main character faces a horrifying decision. Arrested by the Nazis, Sophie and her two children are sent to Auschwitz. Upon their arrival, a Nazi officer tells Sophie she must choose which child will live and which one will die. When she says she cannot choose, the officer tells a guard to take both children to their deaths. With no option except to save one child, Sophie cries out, "Take my little girl," and watches in utter despair as her daughter is led away screaming.

Sometimes we find ourselves in situations with no good options. We face decisions that require us to make compromises we'd prefer not to make. We grieve over the pain that our choices will cause others. And then we despair. A young woman named Bathsheba found herself in such a situation. As we will see through her story, sometimes when you are in a no-win situation, all you can do is persevere.

Studying

The narrator begins the story of David and Bathsheba by saying, "In the spring of the year, the time when kings go out to battle, ...David stayed in Jerusalem." In between the harvests and plantings and after the early spring rains came the war season in Israel. Apparently, a sort of "gentleman's agreement" existed between various states that reserved a specific time each year for resolving territorial disputes so people could spend the remainder of the year focusing on agriculture.

Although David sent forth his troops under Joab's command, during this particular spring, he himself stayed in Jerusalem, reneging on his kingly duties. One evening, David was restless. He got up, went to the palace rooftop, and began to pace. We are never told what troubled David that night, but his concerns quickly left his mind when he saw a beautiful woman bathing. David had an excellent vantage point from his palace, which was situated at the highest point in the city. The woman was probably in her courtyard using rainwater from her house's cisterns for a bath. In the privacy of her home, under the shadows of early evening, it is unlikely that she even knew anyone was watching her.

When David inquired about the woman's identity, he learned that she was Eliam's daughter and Uriah's wife. Both Eliam and Uriah were members of David's elite guard, so he knew both men well. He also knew that, because Bathsheba was another man's wife, she was off-limits. Apparently David considered himself above the law, however, and, since Eliam and Uriah were off fighting his battles, David seized the opportunity.

The act itself is described tersely in the first half of verse 4: David sent messengers to fetch her, she came, and he lay with her. The narrator says nothing about Bathsheba's feelings. Was she fearful and appalled? Was she flattered by the king's attention? Did she go willingly or did she have no choice? Unfortunately, the text is ambiguous enough that scholars have interpreted Bathsheba both as a victim and as a willing, perhaps even conniving, partner (see, for example Alter, 251, who suggests that Bathsheba was an opportunist, and Nicol, 360–61). However, several elements in the story seem to favor the idea that Bathsheba was a victim rather than a co-conspirator.

First, it is hard to believe that Bathsheba somehow knew David would be restless on that particular night, or that he would see her, conclude she was beautiful, and send for her. Did she somehow foresee the future that he would impregnate her and kill her husband so that she could become a queen? To ascribe this kind of omniscience and manipulative power to a woman who is entirely passive throughout the

Bathsheba means "daughter of an oath." She was the daughter of Eliam and the wife of Uriah, both of whom were members of David's elite army of thirty mighty men (2 Sam 23:34, 39).

Adultery Laws

In the Old Testament, adultery was defined as a man having intercourse with the wife of another man. The violation was against the other man; adultery was not an offense a man committed against a woman. For example, if a married man had intercourse with an unmarried woman (a prostitute, a virgin, a widow), he was not committing adultery because he had not violated the sexual rights of another man (though, in the case of the virgin, the man was obligated to marry the woman, and he could not divorce her, Dt 22:38-29). In the same way, a man who had multiple wives (polygamy) was not considered an adulterer because he was married to all of them.

The punishment for adultery was death for both partners (Lev 20:10; Dt 22:22). Interestingly, a man could accuse his wife of impropriety even if he merely suspected that she had been unfaithful (Num 5:12-31), but a woman could not accuse her husband of adultery.

narrative seems rather disingenuous. Second, David is portrayed as the mastermind and driving force behind the whole affair (11:4; 11:6-15). It is he, not Bathsheba, who is proclaimed guilty in 11:27 and 12:5. Third, when Nathan the prophet condemns David in his parable, Bathsheba is clearly portrayed as an innocent victim of David's abuse of power (12:1-4).

Afterward, Bathsheba returned to her house. Sometime later she sent David a note declaring, "I am pregnant." With nowhere else to turn, Bathsheba was forced to contact David for assistance. Uriah was clearly not the father, and when he returned home and found her pregnant, by law he could have her stoned. The only person who could exonerate Bathsheba was David.

The verses that follow (11:6-25) describe how David responded. Rather than taking responsibility for his sin, David instead launched a series of initiatives designed to cover up what he had done. He sent for Uriah on the pretense of asking him to report on the battle's progress. He told the soldier to go home, hoping Uriah would sleep with Bathsheba and conclude that the baby was his own. When Uriah refused on moral grounds, David got him drunk, thinking alcohol would wash Uriah's ethics away. But when Uriah passed out on the palace steps, David coldly plotted the man's demise, writing the murderous instructions to Joab and placing them in Uriah's own hands.

The narrator only briefly describes Bathsheba's grief over Uriah's death, but the words highlight the intimate relationship they shared: "And the *wife of Uriah* heard that Uriah, *her husband*, was dead. And she mourned over *her lord*" (v. 26, author's translation). Bathsheba had lost a husband who truly loved her (2 Sam 12:3), but now she was a widow—and pregnant with the baby of her husband's murderer.

After the prescribed seven-day period of mourning ended (see Gen 50:10), David wasted no time in sending for Bathsheba. In what we might call a "shotgun wedding," he married her, and soon thereafter the baby was born. Once again, we are left to wonder how Bathsheba felt. Was she relieved that she now had a future? Was she devastated to marry the man who had killed her husband? Was the baby a sign of hope for her or a reminder of her shame? Unfortunately, we can only speculate.

David, however, seemed pleased with the outcome of events. By marrying Bathsheba, he thought he had neatly covered his sins, and now he had a baby boy he could call his own. But in an ominous note, the narrator hints at devastating events to come, for "the thing that David had done displeased the LORD." Literally, it was "evil in the Lord's eyes."

Understanding

One can only wonder how much slander Bathsheba endured. The public nature of her summons to David's palace, the scandal of her pregnancy while Uriah was away, the unusual circumstances surrounding Uriah's death, the hurried marriage as soon as the mourning period was over—just one of these events provided enough fodder for gossip. Indeed, even today some people continue to denigrate Bathsheba, accusing her of being at least a seductress, and, at worst, a conniving and power-hungry king-stalker (see, for example, Alter, 251; Nicol, 360-61)!

> Be more concerned with your character than your reputation. Your character is what you really are while your reputation is merely what others think you are.
> —John Wooden

Bathsheba was as much a victim of circumstances as she was the victim of David's lust. It was not her fault that her husband was away fighting battles. She could not help the fact that she was beautiful. She did not choose to be ogled by David (though some interpreters disagree). She could do nothing to prevent pregnancy. Her circumstances and David's actions combined to put her in a horrible and dangerous situation.

In Israel's patriarchal society, Bathsheba had few available options. Had David not married her, she would have been a destitute pregnant widow. Probably, considering the circumstances surrounding her pregnancy, she would have been an outcast. As horrifying as it must have been to marry her husband's murderer, Bathsheba did what was necessary to survive. Bathsheba was stuck between a rock and a hard place, and despite her powerlessness, she found a way through.

What About Me?

• *Where can I turn when I am powerless?* Like Bathsheba, sometimes we find ourselves in situations in which we feel powerless. Unlike Bathsheba, however, most of us have basic legal rights and access to resources to help us in our times of need.

Often, the first step out of powerlessness is asking for help, and our most important resources are our family, friends, and church. Family and friends can offer us a sense of stability and hope merely by being there for us. The church can attend to our spiritual needs, helping us to seek God when we face dark times. Depending on our situation, we can also seek assistance from other sources to help with our finances (accountants, debt counseling), addictions (counseling, self-help groups), relationships (marriage and family resources), and general health (health clinics, basic human services).

• *How should I respond when people judge me for the decisions I felt I had to make?* Sometimes other people judge us harshly when we're in the midst of a difficult situation. They might tell us how we should have dealt with the problem. They might suggest that God is punishing us for not being faithful enough. Unfortunately, we can't control what others think or say about us. However, we can choose how we respond by politely ignoring insensitive comments, respectfully correcting misconceptions, and humbly acknowledging our mistakes. Ultimately, we should be more concerned about finding healing from our past than garnering the approval of others.

• *How can I learn to accept my circumstances?* Living in less-than-ideal circumstances is no easy task, but it may be all we can do, at least for a while. We may have to learn to ask for help from others. We may have to accept a different standard of living. We may have to work together with people we don't like very much. We may have to give up dreams. But accepting circumstances doesn't mean we have to remain forever locked in them. Eventually, we may find a path through our "no-win" situation, so we should always be on the alert to new possibilities. In Christ, we find forgiveness and healing, so we can look toward the future with hope, knowing that circumstances can be redeemed.

Resources

Robert Alter, *The David Story: A Translation with Commentary of 1 and 2 Samuel* (New York: W. W. Norton & Co., 1999).

Ludwig Koehler and Walter Baumgartner, *The Hebrew and Aramaic Lexicon of the Old Testament*, trans. M. E. J. Richardson (Leiden: Brill, 2001) 763.

George G. Nicol, "Bathsheba, a Clever Woman?" *Expository Times* 99 (1988): 360–63.

THE ADULTRESS?

2 Samuel 11:2-5, 26-27a

Introduction

We know Bathsheba first and most graphically from the sexually charged encounter with David in 2 Samuel 11, but the little we know pales in comparison with what we don't know. Should we think of Bathsheba as a seductress or willing accomplice with David, as many do, or was the wife of Uriah a helpless victim of royal rape?

We'll explore those questions in good time, but first, let's appraise what little we know about the mystery woman's background.

Bathsheba's Pedigree (11:3b)

War in the ancient East was often a seasonal affair, and the narrator of 1-2 Samuel is careful to relate that, "in the spring of the year when kings go out to battle" (11:1), David remained in Jerusalem and entrusted the army to Joab, assigning himself the duty of an afternoon nap on the rooftop patio of his palace. The story in which Bathsheba first appears begins with a king who is neglecting his duties and easily distracted.

Rising from his siesta, David turns to voyeurism, spying on a beautiful woman as she takes a ritual bath in the inner courtyard of a nearby home. Many homes of the period consisted of a series of rooms arranged around an open courtyard where cooking fires, clay ovens, storage cisterns, and plastered baths might be found.

The first thing we learn about Bathsheba is her great beauty. Bathsheba's beauty must have been remarkable to draw the king's attention, for David already had a sizeable harem of both wives and concubines (2 Sam 3:2-5, 13-16; 5:13-16). He should not have been troubled by a frustrated libido or a lack of attractive women at his beck and call.

Yet, David liked what he saw of Bathsheba, whom he presumably did not know. When he inquired about her identity, he was told, "This is Bathsheba daughter of Eliam, the wife of Uriah the Hittite."

The double identification of relationships, along with the proximity of Bathsheba's home to the king's residence, suggests that she was a person of considerable status. The name "Bathsheba" could mean "daughter of Sheba," "daughter of an oath," or even "daughter of seven." Was she born following a parent's oath, or as a seventh child? We have no way of knowing.

The little that we do know relates to Bathsheba's father and husband: she is the daughter of someone named Eliam and the husband of "Uriah the Hittite." A list of David's most noted soldiers includes both "Eliam the son of Ahithophel the Gilonite" and "Uriah the Hittite" as belonging to the elite corps known as "the thirty" (2 Sam 23:34-39). The father of the Eliam in 2 Samuel 11:3 is not mentioned, however, so we don't know if this same Eliam was Bathsheba's father. Ahithophel the Gilonite was one of David's most trusted counselors until he switched his loyalty to Absalom (2 Sam 15:12, 31). Bathsheba would have been David's wife by then, however. If Ahithophel's granddaughter was David's wife, it seems unlikely that he would have turned against David.

The more certain identification is that of Bathsheba's husband, Uriah. A fascinating aspect of the story is that Uriah has a good Yahwistic name—"my light is Yahweh"—but is identified as a Hittite. The Hittites' original homeland was in central Anatolia, but their presence in Canaan is attested from the time of the patriarchs (Gen 23:10; 25:9; 26:34). Though ethnically Hittite, it is unlikely that Uriah was a first-generation immigrant.

The identification of Bathsheba's family connections makes David's lechery even more ominous: the woman he plans to take is married to a man who has devoted (and risked) his life in David's service.

This is the second thing we learn about Bathsheba: she is a married woman and should be off-limits to David.

Bathsheba's Summons (11:1-3a, 4)

David sent for Bathsheba, "and she came to him, and he lay with her" (11:4). The text gives no hint as to whether Uriah's wife came willingly or under duress, quickly or hesitantly. We assume she would have felt little choice but to accept the king's invitation, but we don't know how she felt about it.

Does the text speak from silence? It does not say that he forced himself upon her, as Amnon is said to have done in raping his sister Tamar (13:14), but uses a common euphemism for sexual intercourse: "he lay with her."

Whether Bathsheba cried out with alarm, silently endured, or welcomed the illicit interlude is not stated. Was she sickened by David's behavior? We don't know. Was she tired of a Hittite husband who was often away from home on the king's business? We don't know. The only additional information we are given is a parenthetical note with reference to the bath David had observed: "Now she was purifying herself after her period."

Ancient Israel had strict rules regarding purity. Like their ancient neighbors, the Israelites regarded a woman to be ritually unclean during her menstrual period. Cultic regulations decreed that a menstruating woman was considered unclean for seven days, and that anyone who touched her was likewise unclean (Lev 15:19-24). One who had intercourse with a woman during her menses was also considered unclean for seven days afterward.

The narrator's note suggests to us that Bathsheba was observant in following the rituals of purification, though we cannot know if her motivation was personal piety or cultural conformity.

The note also indicates that Bathsheba had emerged from her seven days of sexual quarantine; thus, David would not risk becoming ritually unclean from contact with her. This does not make his actions justified: the law was also clear in declaring that adultery was punishable by death (Lev 20:10; Deut 22:22). David seems to have felt that he was above the law. Perhaps he presumed that no court in the land would convict him.

The more pertinent thing we learn is that Bathsheba, having completed both physical menstruation and ritual lustrations, is entering a cycle of fertility. Sexual intercourse could lead to conception.

For an affair so steeped in imagined intensity, the narrative account is markedly reserved, as if the telling of it was distasteful and the author wanted to be done with it quickly. Only two active verbs are assigned to Bathsheba. After David's summons, "she came to him," and after he lay with her, "she returned to her house." Nothing is recorded of what Bathsheba said or how she felt about the matter.

Bathsheba Speaks (11:5)

Bathsheba's only words in this story are told indirectly, sent to David by a messenger: "I am pregnant." Is it significant that Bathsheba sent a message to David rather than speaking the word in person? If she had been a seductress or equal partner in lust, would she not have been more inclined to contrive a personal visit? The impersonal nature of the message may suggest that the afternoon tryst was also more businesslike than passionate, a case of being used more than being loved.

Bathsheba's message led to the familiar but unsavory story of how David called Uriah back from the battle in hopes that he would sleep with his wife and thus cover the king's crime. As a good soldier, Uriah obeyed and came to David, even as his wife had come when bidden. As a faithful worshiper of God, however, Uriah declined to sleep with his wife because he had pledged purity during the battle. This frustrated David's primary scheme, leading to a sordid backup plan that involved having Uriah deliver to Joab a sealed message containing his own death warrant.

David told his military chief, "Don't let this thing be evil in your eyes" (11:25), but the narrator pointedly adds, "but the thing David had done was evil in the eyes of the LORD" (11:27b).

Bathsheba Mourns, and Marries (11:26-27a)

Take note that the narrator is careful not to call Bathsheba by her given name: it appears only in response to David's request to know her identity. Elsewhere in 2 Samuel 11, the writer refers to her as "the woman" or "the wife of Uriah." In a sense, this depersonalizes Bathsheba, but it also minimizes any shame that might fall her way. In contrast, David is always called by name, David is the one who acts, David is the one who is guilty. Bathsheba enters the story only as the object of David's desire: she remains "the wife of Uriah."

Uriah's wife "made lamentation" for her husband, the reader learns, and as one would expect. The story is told succinctly, however, with no description of bitter tears or abject loss—again, the reader is left in the dark regarding Bathsheba's true emotional state.

David, no doubt, would have also publicly mourned the loss of his able soldier, even as he had led the mourning for Saul and Jonathan (2 Sam 1) and for Abner (2 Sam 3:31-39). The typical mourning period was seven days (Gen 50:10; 1 Sam 31:13; 1 Chr 10:12).

Knowing that Bathsheba was pregnant, David wasted no time bringing her into the palace when the mourning period ended. With an economy of style that continues to show muted disdain for David's actions, the narrator eschews detail for the minimal facts: "David sent and brought her to his house, and she became his wife, and bore him a son" (11:27a). Again, Bathsheba's feelings about her new situation remain a mystery.

David appears to have succeeded in covering his crime, but the narrator closes with the ominous words, "the thing David had done was evil in the eyes of Yahweh."

Bathsheba's Reputation

Bathsheba has been a frequent subject of artistic expression. In paintings, she is typically nude or semi-nude, often bearing a "come-hither" look. In literature, she has been treated in different ways. During the Middle Ages, she was an iconic image in a misogynist tradition that warned against the dangers of women.

Marbod, bishop of Rennes (c. 1035–1123), wrote, "Countless are the traps which the scheming enemy has set throughout the world's paths and plains: but among them the greatest—and the one scarcely anyone can evade—is woman.... Who led astray David the holy and who led wise Solomon astray with sweet charm so that one turned adulterer and the other committed sacrilege— who but seductive woman?" (*The Book with Ten Chapters*, III.1, 4).

During the Renaissance, with its more positive attitudes toward sensuality, Bathsheba appeared as the subject of erotic poetry in Francis Sabie's "David and Bathsheba" (1596), and as the epitome of beauty in Remy Belleau's *Les Amours de David et de Bersabee* (1572) and George Peele's play, *David and Fair Bethsabe* (1599).

Peele portrays Bathsheba as warning against the danger inherent in her allure:

Let not my beauties fire,
Enflame unstaied desire,
Nor pierce any bright eye
That wandreth lightly. (II. 34-37)

More recent literature gives greater attention to the possibility that Bathsheba was more prey than predator. Gladys Schmitt's historical novel *David the King* (1940) explores the feelings of a woman who has no power to resist the advances of her king. More recently, modern Hebrew author Moshe Shamir's *Kivsat Harash* ("The Poor Man's Lamb," 1956, translated into English as *The Hittite Must Die*, 1964) tells the story from Uriah's point of view and reflects on the abuse of power.

What are modern readers to make of Bathsheba? Was she a willing paramour or a victim of royal rape? We have no certain knowledge. In time, of all David's wives, Bathsheba becomes the one who acts most like a queen. For now, however, the narrator reminds us that she is the wife of Uriah.

Notes

Notes

2

THE MOURNER

2 Samuel 12:15b-25

Central Question

How can I face the sickness and death of a loved one?

Scripture

2 Samuel 12:15b-25 15b The LORD struck the child that Uriah's wife bore to David, and it became very ill. 16 David therefore pleaded with God for the child; David fasted, and went in and lay all night on the ground. 17 The elders of his house stood beside him, urging him to rise from the ground; but he would not, nor did he eat food with them. 18 On the seventh day the child died. And the servants of David were afraid to tell him that the child was dead; for they said, "While the child was still alive, we spoke to him, and he did not listen to us; how then can we tell him the child is dead? He may do himself some harm." 19 But when David saw that his servants were whispering together, he perceived that the child was dead; and David said to his servants, "Is the child dead?" They said, "He is dead." 20 Then David rose from the ground, washed, anointed himself, and changed his clothes. He went into the house of the Lord, and worshiped; he then went to his own house; and when he asked, they set food before him and he ate. 21 Then his servants said to him, "What is this thing that you have done? You fasted and wept for the child while it was alive; but when the child died, you rose and ate food." 22 He said, "While the child was still alive, I fasted and wept; for I said, 'Who knows? The LORD may be gracious to me, and the child may live.' 23 But now he is dead; why should I fast? Can I bring him back again? I shall go to him, but he will not return to me." 24 Then David consoled his wife Bathsheba, and went to her, and lay with her; and she bore a son, and he named him Solomon. The LORD loved him, 25 and sent a message by the prophet Nathan; so he named him Jedidiah, because of the LORD.

Reflecting

I was in our garage sorting through items to donate to the Salvation Army when I came upon the bright red bike saddlebags. They were my dad's. He used to bike to work in Albuquerque, riding from our home in the Northeast Heights all the way to his workplace near the University of New Mexico. I paused, my emotional side wondering how I could give them away and my practical side wondering what on earth I could do with them. The practical side won out, so I went through all the pockets removing old facial tissues, bike maps, and loose change.

But when I pulled out a tube of Chapstick, I collapsed on the floor in tears. The grief, which seemed to come out of nowhere, surprised me. My dad had died several years earlier from esophageal cancer when he was only sixty-three. I thought I had processed my grief. I no longer dreamed about him; I rarely contemplated his harrowing last days. But the Chapstick was a sudden reminder that he was really gone. Dad used Chapstick constantly, and he always carried a tube with him. At the end of each day, he would empty out his pockets and put the loose change and Chapstick tube on his dresser. I can still see it there in my memories.

As I held the little black tube in my hands, grief washed over me. This ointment had touched his lips when they still drew breath. It was like I held a tangible piece of him in my hand—a final fleeting connection to his presence.

Grief affects everyone differently, and each person expresses his or her grief uniquely. Some people weep or cry openly while others reel expressionless under the weight of loss. Anger, confusion, helplessness, and shock are all completely normal ways to deal with sorrow. In the passage today, we will consider how David and Bathsheba dealt with theirs.

Studying

"The LORD struck the child that Uriah's wife bore to David, and it became very ill" (2 Sam 12:15b). In a few short words the narrator reveals a horrifying consequence of David's sin: God made the child mortally ill. Nathan had prophesied that the child would die (12:14), and his words of doom transformed into reality.

The idea that God would kill a baby because of his father's sin is difficult to accept. However, such a view is consistent with the worldview of the writer (or writers) of Samuel. According to Old Testament law, murder was punishable by death—a life for a life (Gen 9:6; Exod 21:12; Lev 24:17; Dt 19:21). Thus, according to the law, David should have been executed for Uriah's murder. In this case, an exception was made: the baby substituted for David. The law codes do not record any provisions allowing substitutes for cold-blooded murderers. Perhaps David's life was spared because of God's covenant with him (2 Sam 7) or because as king he was, in some way, above the law. Regardless, David's baby died to fulfill the requirement of "a life for a life."

The focus of the story immediately turns from the baby back to David. Apparently unwilling to accept Nathan's prophecy without a fight, David did everything he could to change God's mind. He "inquired of the Lord," which probably means he went to a

Where the Dead Abide

The most common name in the Old Testament for the place of the dead is Sheol. Located deep beneath the earth (Dt 32:22, 32; Ps 86:13; Isa 7:11; Ezek 31:14-18), Sheol was a place of darkness (Job 17:13) guarded by gates that prevented escape (Ps 9:13; 107:18; Job 38:17; Isa 38:10) (Lewis, 101–104). In the Old Testament, Sheol and death are interchangeable, thus Sheol may be understood as a state of being rather than as a place (see 1 Sam 2:6; 2 Sam 22:6; Job 7:9; 14:13; 17:13; 17:16; Pss 6:5; 18:5; 30:3; 55:15; 89:48; 116:3; Isa 38:10; Hos 13:14; Jnh 2:2). In addition, Sheol seems to represent the common fate of all humans, whether righteous or wicked (Gen 37:35; 1 Sam 2:6; Job 14:13; 21:13; Ps 30:3). While some scholars argue that only the wicked dwelled in Sheol and righteous people were instead gathered to their fathers (Lewis, 103–104), there is little biblical support for this notion (see, however, Pss 9:17; 49:13-15; Isa 14:9-15). Whether David was referring to Sheol or to reunion with the ancestors when he said, "I shall go to him," is uncertain. In either case, he knew that one day he would join his child in death.

local shrine to entreat God through a prophet. He fasted and prostrated himself on the ground all night. In essence, David interceded on behalf of his baby and begged for God to restore him to health. On the seventh day, in spite of David's supplications, the baby died. Surprising those around him, David immediately arose, refreshed himself, worshiped, and returned home to eat. When asked why he mourned while the child lived but stopped mourning once the child died, he explained that he hoped God would intervene. Once the baby died, there was nothing David could do to intercede on the child's behalf. David concluded, "I shall go to him, but he will not return to me," signifying that one day he would join his child in death.

In verse 24, the story turns briefly to Bathsheba, who is identified by name for the first time since 11:3. As readers, we wonder how she has dealt with her baby's death. Unfortunately, the narrator offers no details, telling us only that David "comforted" her. Presumably, she mourned according to the customs of her times. The typical mourning period in the Old Testament was seven days (Gen 50:10; 1 Sam 31:13; 1 Chr 10:12; see also Judith 16:24; Ecclesiasticus 22:12), though lengthier times of mourning were set aside for prominent figures (Gen 50:3; Num 20:29; Dt 34:8). The basic meaning of the word "mourn" in Hebrew (*sapad*) is "to beat one's breast." Mourners expressed their grief vocally with wailing and crying out (Jer 22:18; 34:5) and physically by ripping clothing, fasting, and donning sackcloth (1 Sam 1:12; 2 Sam 3:31; Jer 4:8; Joel 1:13). Sometimes professional mourners were employed to assist in the ritual expressions of grief (Jer 9:17-22; Amos 5:16). The Old Testament also records funeral elegies sung after the deaths of Saul and Jonathan (2 Sam 1:18-27) and Abner (2 Sam 3:33-34) (see Jacob, 453).

David had intercourse with Bathsheba again, this time as her legitimate husband, and she conceived. When the child was born, David named him Solomon, a name that probably means "peace" (Alter, 262). (Others disagree; see inset box.) God must have seen something special in the child because the narrator states emphatically that God loved him.

God sent Nathan the prophet to announce the divine name for the child: Jedidiah, which means "beloved of the LORD." The fact that God so loved Solomon may help explain why Nathan and Bathsheba later intervened to make Solomon king (see 1 Kgs 1:11-31, the text for next week's lesson). In any case, a story that began with tragedy concludes in hope.

Understanding

The death of David and Bathsheba's first child is disturbing on many levels. The death of any baby is tragic, but the fact that this baby died because God struck him is horrifying. While we can explain the baby's death from the Old Testament perspective of "a life for a life," the idea that God punished the child instead of the father is hard to comprehend. We are forced to ask ourselves whether we believe that God kills children to pay for their parents' sins. Do we worry that, if we somehow fail God, God will take one of our loved ones away from us? The text raises but does not answer these legitimate questions.

Perhaps it is best to keep the Israelite worldview in mind. The writers of the books Joshua–2 Kings present God as the author of *all* events. They portray God throwing stones on fleeing Canaanites, killing more than Israel did with the sword (Josh 10:11), sending an evil spirit on Saul (1 Sam 16:14), and putting lying spirits in the mouths of the prophets to deceive Ahab (1 Kgs 22:20-23). From the writers' perspective, everything that happens is the result of God's direct intervention.

The biblical writers attributed to God things that modern people would attribute to disease, circumstance, bad weather, or human evil. Clearly, these writers saw the death of David's child as a fulfillment of Nathan's prophecy (2 Sam 12:14) and as one of the punishments for David's sin. Even so, should we conclude from this story that God causes every child's death or that God punishes people today by striking down their loved ones?

Certainly some Christians believe that God does, in fact, cause all things—good and bad—to happen even today. Others do not believe that God still sends evil spirits or throws stones from the sky to kill people or puts lying words in peoples' mouths. Therefore, neither do they accept the idea that God kills babies to punish their parents.

Nevertheless, the focus of this story is not so much on the reason for the baby's death as on how David (and to a significantly lesser extent, Bathsheba) responded to the baby's illness and death. David refused to accept that Nathan's prophecy was set in stone. Instead, he fasted, prayed, and beseeched God for mercy on the child. In other words, David refused to lose hope while the child still lived. Once the child died, however, David accepted the tragedy with dignity.

What About Me?

• *What do you believe?* A small group used to meet in our house. The group consisted of young married couples, some with small children. During one of our meetings, several women in the group said they felt certain that God was going to punish them by taking away their children. We spent the entire meeting discussing whether or not God punishes Christians the same way God apparently judged people in the Old Testament. What do you believe and why?

• *How can I deal with the sickness and/or death of a loved one?* Three years ago I returned to my childhood home to take care of my mother who was dying of pancreatic cancer. It was the hardest thing I've ever had to do. I watched her suffer from terrible pain. I witnessed her gradually lose her ability to walk, to talk, and ultimately to breathe. I was helpless—there was nothing I could do to intervene.

Watching a loved one suffer or die absolutely shakes you to your foundations. It forces you to examine your beliefs, your relationships, and yourself. You find yourself clinging to the most basic tenets of your faith. There is no magical solution for coping with the loss of a loved one. Ultimately, all we can do is throw ourselves upon the God of strength and say, "I will come through this with God's help."

• *How can I minister to others who are grieving?* Often, well-meaning Christians try to help those who mourn by saying something "spiritual." We hope that by quoting Scripture or offering a reason for the loss, we will bring comfort to those who suffer. Unfortunately, such efforts often backfire, and, instead of comforting the grieving, we add to their pain. For example, a couple who has just suffered a miscarriage will probably not be comforted by a well-meaning friend who says, "Well, you can always have another child. You're young." Or a wife who has lost her husband in Iraq will probably not agree (in that moment) that "all things work together for good." Indeed, sometimes the best comfort we can offer is our silent support—simply being with our friends and crying with them instead of trying to find words to soothe an incomprehensible loss.

Resources

Robert Alter, *The David Story: A Translation with Commentary of 1 and 2 Samuel* (New York: W. W. Norton & Co., 1999).

E. Jacob, "Mourning," in *The Interpreter's Dictionary of the Bible*, ed. George A. Buttrick (Nashville: Abingdon, 1962), 452–54.

Theodore J. Lewis, "Dead, Abode of the," *Anchor Bible Dictionary*, ed. David Noel Freedman (New York: Doubleday, 1992).

THE MOURNER

2 Samuel 12:15b-25

Introduction

The latter part of 2 Samuel 12 cannot be understood apart from the first section, in which David is severely upbraided by the prophet Nathan. Some time had passed since David had taken Bathsheba and killed her husband, so the prophet was able to catch him off guard with a curious story of an arrogant aristocrat who robbed a poor man of his only lamb, a pet that was dear to his heart.

David erupted in anger at such a "son of death" and pronounced judgment upon him, but then Nathan pointed a sharp finger at the king and said, "You are the man" (v. 7).

Nathan went on to remind David of God's past blessings. He insisted that God would have blessed David even more if he had remained true. Instead, David had stolen Uriah's wife and "killed him with the sword of the Ammonites" (v. 9). As a result, Nathan predicted, trouble would rise from within David's house, and the sword would never depart from it (vv. 10-11).

David confessed his guilt, and Nathan declared that the Lord had "put away" David's sin so that he would not face the death penalty he deserved (v. 13, see Lev 20:10; Deut 22:22). In a tragic twist, however, the prophet declared that the child born to David and Bathsheba would die (v. 14).

Bathsheba's Ill-fated Child (v. 15b)

How are we to understand the death of Bathsheba's baby boy? We note first that the narrator again refuses to call Bathsheba by name; she is "Uriah's wife." In a similar manner, the child remains unnamed: "The LORD struck the child that Uriah's wife bore to David, and it became very ill" (v. 15b).

Perhaps the narrator hopes the near anonymity of the child will soften the sting of Nathan's claim that Yahweh caused the boy's death. The very thought that God would spare guilty David and smite his innocent child is disturbing to any thoughtful reader.

Contemporary believers who view the account through a New Testament lens may find some comfort in imagining the death of Bathsheba's blameless child as a foreshadowing of Christ's death on the cross, an atoning sacrifice so that others might live.

Perhaps—but such an interpretation is implied at best, and would in any case offer cold comfort to the boy's mother. The text offers no indication that David had told Bathsheba about Nathan's baleful oracle, and it would be surprising if he had. All Bathsheba knew was that her first husband was dead, her life was upside down, and the boy she had birthed had no future.

Readers often assume the child was born sickly and lived only seven days, but the earlier birth announcement in 11:27 indicates nothing out of the ordinary with the birth. It is more reasonable to presume that the child enjoyed an indefinite period of health before falling ill when Yahweh "struck the child" in fulfillment of Nathan's prophecy. Thus David would know that the child's death was not an accident of birth, but an act of God.

David's Heartfelt Plea (vv. 16-17)

David's response to the boy's illness left the servants and advisors of the royal household scratching their heads. His behavior is described with a series of active verbs: David *pleaded* with Yahweh for the child's life, *fasted* before Yahweh, *went* in and *lay* all night on the ground, prostrating himself before God, presumably beside the child's bed (v. 16). David's pathetic pleading was so appalling that his advisors exhorted him to straighten up and behave with greater dignity, but he would not heed them (v. 17). The narrator's observation that David refused to come and sit at the royal table indicates that he had abandoned the business of running the country, leaving matters of state and protocol in the hands of others.

The sensitive reader may note what David did *not* do. There is no indication that he sought to comfort Bathsheba or paid her any attention at all. Of course, it's possible that David did show compassion toward Bathsheba, but that was not the narrator's concern: the focus of the story is David.

The servants and counselors who surrounded David lived in a time when infant mortality was high. It was a fact of life that many children died young, so a failing child should cause no great surprise. Perhaps they thought David was overreacting, but David knew something they did not know.

Believing that Yahweh had caused the child's illness as punish-ment for the faults of the father, David hoped that Yahweh could be persuaded to reverse course and bring healing. Thus, as long as the child lived, David prayed.

David's Surprising Reaction (vv. 18-23)

But David's prayers were not answered, at least not in the way he wished. The child died despite David's protestations, and his grief had been so deep that the servants were afraid to tell him. Yet, when he heard them whispering and demanded to know if the child was dead, they were shocked by his response. Instead of collapsing, as they feared, the king immediately changed his behavior. He got up from the floor, bathed and shaved, went back to the table, and went back to work (vv. 18-20).

David seems to have regarded his week of fasting and prayer as mourning enough, even though it came before the child died. The culturally accepted season of grief in Israel was seven days, and that is how long David had prayed for the life of the little one. Now he refused to mourn any longer.

In the eyes of his servants, David's demeanor was upside down. While others were attending to business, he mourned. When the child had died and it was the proper time for mourn-ing, David avoided the ritual and went back to work. This aroused such consternation that his servants dared to reprove him (v. 21).

David's response took his hearers aback: "While the child was still alive, I fasted and wept," he said, "for I said, 'Who knows? The LORD may be gracious to me, and the child may live.' But now he is dead; why should I fast? Can I bring him back again? I shall go to him, but he will not return to me" (vv. 22-23).

Whether David's response was motivated by pragmatism or fatalism, we cannot know. When his self-abasement bore no fruit, did he resign himself to the conclusion that God no longer answered his prayers? Or did he simply make the cold calculation that there was nothing to be gained by further grieving? There is some irony in David's behavior: his neglect of duty in the previous chapter had started the unhappy cycle of events; now he eschews mourning and embraces business.

Bathsheba's Consolation (vv. 24-25)

One wonders what Bathsheba has been enduring while David gives all his attention to praying for the child. We could imagine a growing resentment, but she appears not to have held a grudge against her new husband. When David returned to business as usual, a part of that business was Bathsheba, and the narrator gives no indication of a cold reception.

The astute reader notes a shift at this point: when David turns his attention to Bathsheba and comforts her, the narrator acknowledges both her name and that she is now David's wife: "Then David consoled his wife Bathsheba, and went to her, and lay with her; and she bore a son, and he named him Solomon" (v. 24).

Despite its unhappy beginning, the marriage between David and Bathsheba is now regarded as legitimate, and the same God who had struck their first child now dotes on the second: "The LORD loved him."

In one of strangest twists in the Bible, the birth story of the acclaimed King Solomon emerges from the dark shadow of Nathan's curse. Yahweh did not answer David's plea to save the first child, but God's grace was expressed in the granting of another son, a son clearly favored by God.

The books of 1–2 Samuel, along with other narrative accounts in Joshua–2 Kings, probably reached their final form during the exile. Later readers would need to hear that there is hope, even in the midst of darkness. A new son was born, and "The LORD loved him."

While Bathsheba's first child goes unnamed, her second son receives two names. Naming children seems to have been a mother's prerogative during the period (1 Sam 1:20; 4:21), but it is unclear whether David or Bathsheba gave him the name Solomon: the Masoretic Text has "he called his name," but other textual traditions have the feminine form of the verb.

Solomon's name is derived from the Hebrew root *sh-l-m*. The noun form is often translated as "peace," but its underlying meaning is one of wholeness, completeness, or well-being. Thus, the name "Shlomo" (its Hebrew pronunciation) may mean "man of peace," as indicated by 1 Chronicles 22:9, or possibly "one who makes complete," perhaps in the sense of "replacement."

Surprisingly, a second name was given to the child, reportedly by Yahweh himself. The prophet Nathan declared that he should be called "Jedidiah," a name that literally means "Beloved One of Yahweh." One might think a divinely decreed name would override the parents' wishes, but this name does not appear again in the Bible. Some have suggested that Jedidiah may have been used as a throne name, but there is no evidence for it: the child is always known as Solomon.

Although Solomon's birth story is brief, it is in sharp contrast to that of his ill-fated brother. Bathsheba's first son was unlawfully conceived, unnamed by the biblical writer, and unfortunate—crushed by the weight of his father's sin. In contrast, Solomon is born within a marriage now deemed legitimate, twice named, and beloved by Yahweh. Solomon is destined for great things, and Bathsheba is his mother.

How does Bathsheba feel about this? Is she resigned to being the wife of the king, or delighted by her elevation to royalty? We don't know.

Is she resentful of David's inward turn during the child's illness and his refusal to mourn after his death? We don't know.

Does she welcome David's consolation and the resumption of their sexual relations? We don't know.

Is she comforted by the birth of a second son? Here we can be a bit more confident about a positive answer. The text has little to say about Bathsheba's ongoing relationship with David, but in time she became a strong advocate for her son Solomon, the subject of our next lesson.

Notes

Notes

3

THE ADVOCATE

1 Kings 1:11-31

Central Question

Whom can I help through my advocacy?

Scripture

1 Kings 1:11-31 11 Then Nathan said to Bathsheba, Solomon's mother, "Have you not heard that Adonijah son of Haggith has become king and our lord David does not know it? 12 Now therefore come, let me give you advice, so that you may save your own life and the life of your son Solomon. 13 Go in at once to King David, and say to him, 'Did you not, my lord the king, swear to your servant, saying: Your son Solomon shall succeed me as king, and he shall sit on my throne? Why then is Adonijah king?' 14 Then while you are still there speaking with the king, I will come in after you and confirm your words." 15 So Bathsheba went to the king in his room. The king was very old; Abishag the Shunammite was attending the king. 16 Bathsheba bowed and did obeisance to the king, and the king said, "What do you wish?" 17 She said to him, "My lord, you swore to your servant by the LORD your God, saying: Your son Solomon shall succeed me as king, and he shall sit on my throne. 18 But now suddenly Adonijah has become king, though you, my lord the king, do not know it. 19 He has sacrificed oxen, fatted cattle, and sheep in abundance, and has invited all the children of the king, the priest Abiathar, and Joab the commander of the army; but your servant Solomon he has not invited. 20 But you, my lord the king—the eyes of all Israel are on you to tell them who shall sit on the throne of my lord the king after him. 21 Otherwise it will come to pass, when my lord the king sleeps with his ancestors, that my son Solomon and I will be counted offenders." 22 While she was still speaking with the king, the prophet Nathan came in. 23 The king was told, "Here is the prophet Nathan." When he came in before the king, he did obeisance to the king, with his face to the ground. 24 Nathan said, "My lord the king, have you said, 'Adonijah shall succeed me as king, and he shall sit on my throne'? 25 For today he has gone down and has sacrificed oxen, fatted cattle, and sheep in abundance, and has invited all the king's children, Joab the commander of the army, and the priest Abiathar, who are now eating and drinking before him, and saying, 'Long live King Adonijah!' 26 But he did not invite me, your servant, and the priest Zadok, and Benaiah son of Jehoiada, and your servant Solomon. 27 Has this thing been brought about by my lord the king and you have not let your servants know who should sit on the throne of my lord the king after him?" 28 King David answered, "Summon Bathsheba to me." So she came into the king's presence, and stood before the king. 29 The king swore, saying, "As the LORD lives, who has saved my life from every adversity, 30 as I swore to you by the LORD, the God of Israel, 'Your son Solomon shall succeed me as king, and he shall sit on my throne in my place,' so will I do this day." 31 Then Bathsheba bowed with her face to the ground, and did obeisance to the king, and said, "May my lord King David live forever!"

Reflecting

Political wrangling is nothing new. Power plays, underhanded tactics, and ruthless maneuvering were just as common in ancient times. Political savvy helped a person gain power, but more often than not people got ahead in politics through their personal connections. Just as political endorsements can make or break a candidate today, so it was in ancient Israel. Knowing the right people could determine one's political future.

Because we know Solomon became king after David, we often assume his succession to the throne was a given. But according to 1 Kings 1:1-10, the question of who would follow David was anything but clear. David's death was imminent, but he had not named a successor. Consequently, confusion erupted. David's son Adonijah made a legitimate claim of kingship.

Adonijah was next in line for the throne. He was David's fourth son, and the previous sons were all dead (2 Sam 3:4; see 2 Sam 13:28-29; 18:14). In addition, Adonijah garnered the support of both Joab, the commander of David's armies, and Abiathar, the high priest (1 Kgs 1:7). Considering Adonijah's birthright and the fact that he had both military and religious support, his claim to the throne was almost incontrovertible. Had Bathsheba and Nathan not intervened in a daring political gambit, Solomon would never have become king.

Studying

When he heard that Adonijah had declared himself king, Nathan the prophet immediately took action. He went straight to Bathsheba, informed her of Adonijah's claim, and alerted her that she and Solomon were in danger. If Adonijah was king, he would likely move to solidify his throne by killing any other contenders. Clearly, Adonijah posed a threat to Bathsheba. But Nathan's motives for intervening in the succession are never stated. It appears that there were at least two political factions vying for power in Jerusalem:

At least two political factions vied for power in 1 Kings 1: Adonijah's group and Solomon' group. Some commentators suggest that Adonijah's group represented a Judean coalition centered at Hebron. This party advocated for the supremacy of Judah and was not interested in maintaining unity between the tribes. The Solomon group represented a Jerusalem-centered coalition that was committed to a united Israel. (See Provan, 24–25; Jones, 91–92.)

Adonijah's group, which included all the men of Judah and David's servants (1 Kgs 1:7, 9), and Nathan's group, which included David's closest military champions and advisors (1 Kgs 1:8; 26). Whoever won the kingship would reward his supporters and subjugate—or eliminate—those in opposition. Thus, Nathan's motives may have included his own self-interest. By helping Bathsheba convince David that Solomon should be king, Nathan secured his own future. Nathan instructed Bathsheba to go to the king first and remind him of his oath to make Solomon king. Subsequently, Nathan said he would arrive and confirm Bathsheba's claims (1 Kgs 1:11-14).

Bathsheba obeyed Nathan's command and went immediately to David's bedroom where he lay as an invalid. She reminded David of an oath, emphasizing that he swore to her by the Lord God that Solomon would be king. Second Samuel does not record an oath declaring Solomon David's successor, so whether David actually made the oath is uncertain. While the Lord's favor for Solomon (2 Sam 12:24-25) certainly set him apart from David's other sons, there is no clear directive in Scripture from either God or David that Solomon would be the next king.

By identifying herself as David's "handmaiden," Bathsheba presented herself as a humble petitioner. Nevertheless, her strong words to David indicate that she was a powerful advocate on behalf of her son. First, Bathsheba apprised David of the political situation: "Adonijah has become king, though you, my lord the king, do not know it" (v. 18). Second, she informed David that Adonijah had sacrificed animals; invited Abiathar, Joab, and others to the feast; but excluded Solomon. Third, she presented the king with a decision he alone could make: "the eyes of all Israel are on you

A Play on Bathsheba's Name

Underlying the story in 1 Kings 1:11-31 is a wordplay not evident in the English translation. Bathsheba's name means "daughter of the oath." In Hebrew, the word for oath is *sheba'* and the word "to swear an oath" comes from the same root (*shaba'*) "swear." Thus, in verses 13, 17, 29, 30, the similarity between Bathsheba's name and the oath David swore is highlighted. Bathsheba (the "daughter of the oath") pressed David regarding the oath (*sheba'*) which he swore (*shaba'*) to Bathsheba!

to tell them who shall sit on the throne of my lord the king after him." In a final climactic plea, Bathsheba told David of the threat to her life and Solomon's if he failed to act (v. 21). Bathsheba appealed to David's sense of honor and justice.

Then Nathan entered and Bathsheba apparently left the room. Bowing before the king, Nathan presented his version of the events, following the exact same order as Bathsheba's report. However, in his retelling, Nathan included the detail that Adonijah excluded not only Solomon, but Zadok, Benaiah, and himself. Avoiding any mention of the oath that was so central to Bathsheba's plea, Nathan instead accused David of failing to inform his closest advisors that he had made Adonijah king. Nathan appealed to David's sense of loyalty to his supporters.

Convinced, David called for Bathsheba to return to the room and confirmed that he had sworn Solomon would be king. Reiterating the words of the oath, David made it a reality: "so will I do this day."

In response, Bathsheba blessed David: "May my lord King David live forever." Considering that David was on his deathbed, he obviously would not live forever. But Bathsheba's blessing was genuine in the sense that David would live on forever through his progeny—progeny who would now descend from Bathsheba's son, Solomon.

Understanding

Readers are sometimes surprised to find "politicking" in the Bible. They imagine, perhaps, that leaders arrived at their positions because God chose them beforehand or because they earned their stripes in battle. Sometimes that is the case, but often we discover that "politics as usual" happened in Old Testament Israel just as it does today.

Adonijah had all the right qualifications for succeeding his father David. He was next in line for the throne, he was supported by powerful people, and he took the initiative to offer leadership in the vacuum created by David's frailty. But in his prideful assumption of kingship, Adonijah underestimated one thing. As weak as he was, David was still king, and what Adonijah lacked was David's stamp of approval.

Bathsheba and Nathan, however, understood the power of kingly endorsement. Thus, they advocated on behalf of Solomon by going to the one person who could definitively name the next king. Appealing to David's sense of honor and loyalty, both Bathsheba and Nathan convinced the ailing king that Solomon should succeed him. Regardless of whether or not David had indeed sworn an oath to Bathsheba, persuasion ultimately overruled power politics, and Solomon became king.

> **Definition of "Advocate"**
> 1: one that pleads the cause of another; *specifically*: one that pleads the cause of another before a tribunal or judicial court
> 2: one that defends or maintains a cause or proposal
> 3: one that supports or promotes the interests of another (Webster's Online Dictionary)

What About Me?

• *Do I try to take advantage of the weaknesses of others?* One of the most disturbing aspects of Adonijah's claim for the throne was that he took advantage of David's weakness. He saw an opportunity for his own advancement and took it instead of going to David and humbly asking for the king's blessing. We want to believe that we never take advantage of others, but we must consider the possibility. For instance, do I tip a waitress less, even if her service is exemplary, because she's of a different ethnicity? Do I take advantage of my boss's "keep your own hours" policy by coming in late and leaving early? Do I constantly look for loopholes and try to beat the system just because I can?

• *Who should be an advocate?* Sometimes situations demand that we intervene on behalf of another. Perhaps a teacher at school is treating one of our children unfairly. As parents, it is our duty to become advocates for our children. Perhaps a coworker has become the object of gossip or backstabbing at work. As Christians, shouldn't we speak against slander? Perhaps we suspect that a friend's husband is abusing her. As difficult as it might be to contact the proper authorities, we must be advocates for those who are in danger.

• *How can we be a good advocate?* We can learn from Nathan and Bathsheba's advocacy for Solomon. First, both Bathsheba and Nathan approached David with humility. Being deferential and humble can help to diffuse a tense situation. Second, Bathsheba and Nathan described the situation carefully and clearly explained what they wanted from David. Clear communication and well-defined goals make for a much stronger case. Third, when David granted Bathsheba's request, she expressed gratitude. Obviously, if our advocacy is successful we should respond graciously.

Resources

G. H. Jones, *1 and 2 Kings*, vol. 1, The New Century Bible Commentary, ed. Ronald E. Clements (Grand Rapids: Eerdmans, 1984).

Iain W. Provan, *1 and 2 Kings*, The New International Biblical Commentary (Peabody MA: Hendrickson, 1995).

Webster's Online Dictionary, http://www.merriamwebster.com/dictionary/advocate.

THE ADVOCATE

1 Kings 1:11-31

Introduction

We are all familiar with parents who are constant advocates for their children. Supporting our children is a good thing, but when parents lobby their daughter's teachers for better grades or pressure their son's coach to make him the starting quarterback, they've gone from advocacy to interference.

Today's text speaks of a time when Bathsheba went to bat for her son. Together with the prophet Nathan, Bathsheba had high hopes for Solomon, and they went far beyond being captain of the team. She wanted David to make her son king. Bathsheba was a skilled negotiator and knew her husband well. She did not pester the king with her request, but when she spoke, he listened.

Our designated text for this session is 1 Kings 1:11-31, but to understand the playing field, we need a scouting report from vv. 1-10.

Adonijah's Ambition (1:1-10)

Solomon faced both stiff competition and a balky coach on the path to kingship. As David grew in age and declined in health, it became obvious that a successor should be designated and prepared to take over at the appointed time. Yet, according to the historian responsible for 1 Kings, David had made no public preparations. The transition to his successor would be the first time a king in Israel had prospects of dying a natural death, and the rule of primogeniture had not yet been established, so there was natural uncertainty about who would inherit the throne.

Despite his age, David had declined—or neglected—to appoint a successor. Both he and Saul, his predecessor, had been called out and confirmed by the elders of Israel and Judah, so David may not have assumed that he had authority to name the next king. Indeed, the chapter opens with a reminder of how extensively David had withdrawn from active life.

David is described as having become so old and frail that "he could not get warm." While this may intend nothing more than a constant case of the shivers, the inability to "get warm" may be a euphemism indicating that David was no longer virile. A country-wide search turned up a beautiful young woman from Shunem who was appointed to be David's private nurse, with duties that included lying "in his bosom" so the king might "be warm." The woman's name was Abishag, and she was given the status of a royal concubine, though the text carefully notes that David did not engage in sexual relations with her. The implication is that David had become sexually as well as politically impotent (1:1-4).

The reader is left to wonder why Bathsheba was not keeping David warm at night. Had their relationship cooled with the passing of the years? Or did palace protocol maintain a separation between the king and his harem, as in the later story of Esther? Was it by choice that Bathsheba no longer slept with the king? As with most questions relative to our heroine's inner thoughts or personal life, we do not know.

While David was caught up in his illness, others were vying for his job. Adonijah was David's fourth-born son, and presumably the next in line to succeed him. His older brothers Amnon and Absalom had both died violent deaths, and his brother Chileab (mentioned only in 2 Sam 3:2-4 as the son of Abigail) was either deceased or a non-factor.

As David delayed in naming a successor, Adonijah decided to follow his older brother Absalom's earlier lead. Ignoring the reigning king, he gathered a contingent of government leaders who would proclaim him as the new ruler. A comparison of Absalom's coup de'état (2 Sam 15–16) and Adonijah's actions in verses 5-10 reveal pointed similarities. Both set their plan in motion by hiring chariots, horsemen, and professional body-guards, seeking respect through the accouterments of royalty.

Surely David would have been informed of Adonijah's presumptive activities, but he did nothing about it, just as he had ignored Absalom's earlier rebellion. In the latter half of 2 Samuel, the narrator portrays David as a distant parent who is overly lenient with his troublesome sons. Now he appears to be senile as well.

As Adonijah took on the affectations of kingship, Solomon resurfaced for the first time since the brief story of his birth in 2 Samuel 12:24-25. As a rival to Adonijah, Solomon also gained a solid base of support, and two parties developed with powerful advocates on each side.

Adonijah's party was composed of traditionalists: David's long-time general Joab defected to his cause, as did Abiathar, who had served as David's priest from the time he left Saul's court and later served as high priest.

Those who remained loyal to David (and ultimately Solomon) were equally faithful but less deeply rooted in the Israelite establishment. These included Abiathar's rival Zadok, whom David had appointed as co-high priest after establishing his capital in Jerusalem, and Benaiah, who commanded the "Cherethites and Pelethites," mercenary forces who served as the king's personal security detail (2 Sam 8:18). Solomon also had support from Nathan, the prophet who had declared Yahweh's special love for him (2 Sam 12:25). The coalition was strengthened by the little-known but apparently significant personages Shimei and Rei, and by David's most loyal warriors, known as his "mighty men."

Matters came to a head when Adonijah called his followers together "by the stone Zoheleth, which is beside En-rogel" (v. 9), a prominent spring not far from Jerusalem. Adonijah invited most of his brothers and his coterie of backers, but pointedly excluded Solomon and his supporters. Adonijah "sacrificed sheep, oxen, and fatted cattle" for the feast, which was clearly intended to be a coronation banquet.

Bathsheba's Advocacy (1:11-27)

Bathsheba enters the picture with Nathan's approach in verse 11. Nathan recognized that Bathsheba still had a position of influence with David and asked her to intervene with the king on Solomon's behalf. Once Adonijah had effectively declared himself king, Nathan realized that Solomon and his supporters were in danger, as it was not unusual in the ancient Near East for a new king to execute any opposition.

Colluding with Bathsheba, Nathan set in motion a plan to win David's support for Solomon, an act played out in five scenes. First, the prophet met with Bathsheba to inform David of Adonijah's actions. He bade her visit the king and follow a predetermined script, asking David if he remembered having previously sworn to appoint Bathsheba's son Solomon to succeed him (vv. 11-13). Nathan would then enter to confirm Bathsheba's reminder that David had promised the throne to Solomon (v. 14).

The Bible contains no prior record of such a promise, so some scholars suppose that Nathan and Bathsheba took advantage of David's lessened capacities by inventing the reported oath and devising a two-stage strategy to convince David that he had sworn it. Whether David was duped or truthfully reminded is unclear, however. He appears mentally sharp when he receives the news that Adonijah had claimed the throne.

Scene two begins with careful attention to royal protocol as Bathsheba approaches David and Abishag, who is attending him. Rather than rushing in, she "bowed and did obeisance to the king," waiting for him to ask why she had come (vv. 15-16). Only then did Bathsheba speak, using her own intuition to adapt Nathan's question-based script.

Consistently addressing the king as "my lord," Bathsheba did not ask if David remembered designating Solomon, but stated it as a firm fact, insisting that he had sworn the oath in Yahweh's name (v. 17). She then informed him of Adonijah's self-coronation (vv. 18-19) and called upon David to exert his authority: "But you, my lord the king—the eyes of all Israel are on you to tell them who shall sit on the throne of my lord the king after him" (v. 20).

Appealing to David's affection, Bathsheba reminded him that, should Adonijah succeed in becoming king, both she and Solomon would be "counted as offenders" and thus placed in mortal jeopardy after David's death (v. 21).

According to plan, Nathan entered (scene three) and vouchsafed Bathsheba's account, reinforcing her claim with his own recollection. Nathan followed Bathsheba's example of prostrating himself, but reverted to his preferred approach of engaging the king through loaded questions: "My lord the king, have you said, 'Adonijah shall succeed me as king, and he shall sit on my throne'?" (v. 24). Nathan described the usurper's activities (vv. 25-26) and asked, "Has this thing been brought about by my lord the king and you have not let your servants know who should sit on the throne of my lord the king after him?" (v. 27). Nathan's pointed words were designed to do far more than raise questions. They also obliquely criticized the king for seeming to have endorsed Adonijah without seeking the prophet's (and therefore God's) advice.

David's Directions (vv. 28-31)

The twin appeals to David's sense of command had their desired effect. As scene four unfolds, the aged monarch rallies from his sickbed with restored royal vigor. He calls for Bathsheba, who had apparently left when Nathan entered, and swears in her presence an even stronger oath that Solomon will reign after him (vv. 28-30).

David's desire to declare his intention directly to Bathsheba suggests strong respect. The king could have spoken only to Nathan, and one would expect him to summon other high officials or a court recorder for the pronouncement. Instead, it seems that the person he wanted most to hear his declaration was Bathsheba, the object of his former passion, the mother of his son Solomon, the wife whose opinion he valued.

Bathsheba responded with another round of bowing and scraping before the elderly king, declaring, "May my lord King David live forever!" (v. 31). The sincerity of Bathsheba's wish may be suspect, but her advocacy had achieved its purpose: if not for her intervention, the history of Israel might have gone in a different direction, and the famed King Solomon would never have taken the throne.

Energized by the emergency, David (who understood the power of pomp and circumstance) issued a string of commands that are played out in a final scene. First, he instructed Nathan to put Solomon on the king's own mule and take him along with Benaiah and Zadok to Gihon, another spring on the outskirts of

Jerusalem, but nearer the main city than En-Rogel. There Nathan was to officially anoint Solomon as king with special oil taken from the sacred tent that housed the Ark of the Covenant.

With the Cherethites and Pelethites along for security, Zadok and Benaiah carried out David's command, formally declaring Solomon to be the next king. The blowing of horns and cheers of the people were such that Adonijah and his company could hear it, causing quick consternation. Adonijah realized that his play for power had come to naught, and he was now in danger of being killed as a potential rival. As his supporters fled, Adonijah sought refuge by taking hold of the horns of the sacred altar, a traditional way of requesting asylum (Exod 21:12-14). Solomon responded to his appeal with an oath that no harm would come to him if he proved to be loyal, however, and sent him home in peace.

This story of virility and violence, of political maneuvering and palace intrigue would not be known to us if not for the account in 1 Kings: the version told in 1 Chronicles 23 and 29 makes no mention of David's infirmity or of Bathsheba's involvement. In the Chronicler's version David is strong, in charge, and taking the initiative throughout. First Kings 1 offers the spiritual descendants of Israel a larger picture—the picture of a mother whose actions changed history.

Notes

Notes

4

THE INTERCESSOR?

1 Kings 2:13-25

Central Question

What is my responsibility toward those who make foolish choices?

Scripture

1 Kings 2:13-25 13 Then Adonijah son of Haggith came to Bathsheba, Solomon's mother. She asked, "Do you come peaceably?" He said, "Peaceably." 14 Then he said, "May I have a word with you?" She said, "Go on." 15 He said, "You know that the kingdom was mine, and that all Israel expected me to reign; however, the kingdom has turned about and become my brother's, for it was his from the LORD. 16 And now I have one request to make of you; do not refuse me." She said to him, "Go on." 17 He said, "Please ask King Solomon—he will not refuse you—to give me Abishag the Shunammite as my wife." 18 Bathsheba said, "Very well; I will speak to the king on your behalf." 19 So Bathsheba went to King Solomon, to speak to him on behalf of Adonijah. The king rose to meet her, and bowed down to her; then he sat on his throne, and had a throne brought for the king's mother, and she sat on his right. 20 Then she said, "I have one small request to make of you; do not refuse me." And the king said to her, "Make your request, my mother; for I will not refuse you." 21 She said, "Let Abishag the Shunammite be given to your brother Adonijah as his wife." 22 King Solomon answered his mother, "And why do you ask Abishag the Shunammite for Adonijah? Ask for him the kingdom as well! For he is my elder brother; ask not only for him but also for the priest Abiathar and for Joab son of Zeruiah!" 23 Then King Solomon swore by the Lord, "So may God do to me, and more also, for Adonijah has devised this scheme at the risk of his life! 24 Now therefore as the LORD lives, who has established me and placed me on the throne of my father David, and who has made me a house as he promised, today Adonijah shall be put to death." 25 So King Solomon sent Benaiah son of Jehoiada; he struck him down, and he died.

Reflecting

I'm not a fan of horror movies. I don't like to be scared, and I definitely don't enjoy being spooked by sudden noises, screams, and creepy music. But what I hate most is watching the characters in the movie do stupid things. It's dark and someone dangerous is lurking about. The protagonist awakens to a sound downstairs. What does she do? Turn on the lights? Call the police? Lock the bedroom door? Hightail it to the neighbor's house? No, of course not. She walks slowly down the shadowy stairway right toward the source of the sound while squeaky violins crescendo.

The whole time I'm thinking, "Don't do it! Stop! Turn around. Run!" But I know it's inevitable. She pushes the door open and there's Horrible Harry with his butcher knife waiting for her. I always scream out loud as if I didn't see it coming.

The account in 1 Kings 2 of Adonijah's demise is a horror story. After his failed attempt to take the throne, Adonijah's supporters abandoned him, and he was forced to flee to the altar to plead for mercy. Solomon allowed Adonijah to live—but with one provision: "If he proves to be a worthy man, not one of his hairs shall fall to the ground; but if wickedness is found in him, he shall die" (1 Kgs 1:52).

As readers, we can see it coming: Adonijah won't prove worthy. Something wicked lurks within him, and Solomon stands at the bottom of the stairs with his knife sharpened.

What do you do when you see someone about to make a terrible mistake? What do you wish you could do?

Studying

Solomon was David's eighth-born son, and thus far down the line of succession. How did he managed to become king? David's first six sons were born to six different wives. His first son, Amnon, was killed by David's third son, Absalom, in retaliation for Amnon's rape of Absalom's sister—his own half-sister. Absalom was later killed in battle when he had launched a rebellion against his father. David's second son, Chileab, is only mentioned in genealogical lists and is supposed to have died at an early age. The same is apparently also true for David's fifth and sixth sons, Shephatiah and Ithream. David's seventh son was the son of Bathsheba who died in infancy. Thus, at the end of David's reign, only Adonijah, the fourth-born son of David, stood between Solomon and the throne (see 2 Sam 3:2-5; 1 Chr 3:1-9).

Adonijah sought an audience with Bathsheba, Solomon's mother. In Israel, mothers of the kings held a special position of honor. This is demonstrated by the fact that in sixteen succession notices of the Judahite kings, the name of the king's mother is recorded (1 Kgs 14:21; 15:2, 10; 2 Kgs 8:26; 12:1; 14:2; 15:2, 33; 18:2; 21:1, 19; 22:1, 31; 23:36; 24:8, 18). The royal treatment Solomon gave to Bathsheba (1 Kgs 2:19) illustrates the honor queen mothers apparently received. While some scholars have argued that queen mothers played a specific political role as advisors and representatives for their sons (Newsome and Ringe, 104), the Old Testament offers limited evidence for such a claim. Even if they held no specific office, however, queen mothers were accorded a special place in the history of the kings.

On the surface, it seems strange that Adonijah sought Bathsheba since she was Solomon's champion. Indeed, when she first saw him she questioned his motives, asking, "Do you come peaceably?" Bathsheba was right to be concerned. After all, had Adonijah become king, both she and Solomon would likely have been executed. But Adonijah reassured her that he came in peace.

> Have you ever purposely failed to intervene because you thought someone's folly would work to your advantage?

Adonijah approached Bathsheba carefully (v. 14), summarizing his loss of the kingdom and interpreting it as the will of God. Whether or not Adonijah believed that God had truly engineered his defeat is unclear. Perhaps he did, or perhaps he was trying to gain Bathsheba's favor. Regardless, he finally voiced his request: "Speak to Solomon, he will not refuse you, so that he may give me Abishag the Shunammite as a wife" (vv. 17-18; author's translation). On the surface, Adonijah's request seems innocent enough.

We know little about Abishag, the young, beautiful virgin who married David in his old age (1 Kgs 1:3). Her name may mean "my father is a wanderer." She was a Shunammite. Shunem was a small town located in Issachar's territory (Josh 19:18). On the eastern edge of the Megiddo plain (Jones, 89), Shunem was where the Philistines gathered against Saul in his last battle (1 Sam 28:4). Abishag was the young virgin given to David to test his virility. Because David was impotent, she remained a virgin even while married to him (1 Kgs 1:4).

The fact that she had remained a virgin is what launched Adonijah's original claim for the throne. But now David was dead—what harm could come from allowing Adonijah to marry Abishag?

While it is possible to conclude that Adonijah's request was innocent—perhaps he had fallen in love with the beautiful virgin—most interpreters believe Adonijah had ulterior motives. In 2 Samuel 16:21, Absalom, another of David's sons, takes over Jerusalem and has intercourse with David's concubines (see also 2 Sam 3:6-7; 12:8). For some reason, in Israel, if a man had sex with a king's wife or concubine, it strengthened his claim to the throne. Since Abishag was David's wife, Adonijah may have asked to marry her in order to launch another campaign for the kingship. Bathsheba agreed to bring Adonijah's request to Solomon,

> Solomon "inherited" his father David's harem as a token of his right to rule in David's place. This custom is an example of how honor was construed in the ancient world in terms of the ability to protect and control one's women. In this context, to sleep with the consort or wife of one's rival constituted a challenge to his honor and authority (Gen 49:3 [cf. Gen 35:22]; 2 Sam 12:8; 16:20-22).

but it is unclear what she thought about the matter. Was Bathsheba unaware that Adonijah's request would amount to a claim for the throne? Did she want to help him by giving him Abishag as a consolation prize? Or did she carry the ill-fated plea to Solomon because she knew how her son would react? Was she hoping that Solomon would consider the request an "unworthy" act and kill Adonijah, thereby securing Solomon's future?

When Bathsheba arrived in Solomon's court, he showed extraordinary deference to her. He bowed before her, prepared a throne for her, and sat her on his right side, the place of honor. Clearly Solomon adored her, and that may be why Adonijah sent Bathsheba as his emissary.

Bathsheba said, "I have one small request.... May Abishag the Shunammite be given to Adonijah, your brother, as a wife."

Solomon responded violently to the request, obviously concluding that Adonijah's intent was treacherous—whether or not it was. Evoking David's final oath (1 Kgs 1:29-30), Solomon swore his own oath, declaring in the Lord's name that before the day was over Adonijah would die. Solomon immediately sent Benaiah to carry out the execution, and Adonijah was quietly and finally silenced.

Understanding

The story in 1 Kings 2 raises all sorts of interesting and troubling questions about the motives of each person involved. Was Adonijah innocently seeking Abishag for a wife, or was he hoping to use her as a basis for reclaiming the throne? Was Bathsheba unaware that Adonijah's request for Abishag could be seen as a treacherous act? Or did she use his request to her advantage, knowing that Solomon would view Adonijah's request as "wickedness"? Did Solomon respond wisely and righteously by executing Adonijah? Or did he transform an innocuous request into treason so he could execute his former rival? Unfortunately, we will never know.

"A wise child makes a glad father, but the foolish despise their mothers" (Prov 15:20).

Nevertheless, the text offers unambiguous insights. For example, it's clear that regardless of Adonijah's motives, his request for Abishag was dangerously foolish. Surely he knew how Solomon might perceive his request, yet he still made it. Sometimes people make foolish choices that lead to devastating consequences.

While Adonijah is the obvious loser in this story, one other victim is overlooked and forgotten. Abishag was a pawn in the political games of the powerful. She was used as human Viagra to test David's virility, a test that led to Adonijah's claim of the kingship. Adonijah requested her as a wife either because he wanted a "consolation prize" after the loss of the kingship or because he saw her as a means by which he could claim the throne. Bathsheba viewed Abishag in a similar light—either as a way to appease Adonijah or as the final nail in Adonijah's coffin. We know nothing of Abishag's fate, but, because she was David's widow, it is likely that she was ensconced in David's household and never allowed to remarry, living out her days as a silent victim of other people's aspirations.

What About Me?

• *Should I speak up if I think someone is making a foolish mistake?* We may perceive that another person is about to make a bad decision. Unfortunately, it's not always clear whether we should try to intervene. In the case of a child, for example, we may need to let the child learn the consequences of, say, eating too much candy or choosing not to do homework. What if a friend is about to make a potentially bad decision? We may have to consider whether our intervention is worth the potential rupture of a friendship. Obviously, the seriousness of the error is the key issue. If my child has decided to experiment with drugs, I should intervene. If my friend refuses to end an abusive relationship, I must intervene—even at the cost of losing the friend.

• *Showing concern for the silent victims.* Who are the Abishags in your life? Can you think of people at your workplace, in your neighborhood, at your church, or in your family who are victims of neglect? Who are the people being ignored, used, or forgotten?

Try to think of at least one person—perhaps a person at work who is taken for granted, a neglected elderly person in your neighborhood, or a child at your kids' school who is bullied. Purposefully reach out to that person. Sometimes the simplest gestures—a smile, calling someone by name, a card, or a hug—can restore the dignity of one who has been ignored.

Resources

G. H. Jones, *1 and 2 Kings*, vol. 1., The New Century Bible Commentary, ed. Ronald E. Clements (Grand Rapids MI: Eerdmans, 1984).

Carol A. Newsom and Sharon H. Ringe, eds., *Women's Bible Commentary*, expanded ed. (Louisville: Westminster/John Knox, 1998).

THE INTERCESSOR?

1 Kings 2:13-25

Introduction

Perhaps you know people who are hard to read. They might appear sincere, but you never know what feelings, thoughts, plans, or schemes might lie (or lurk) beneath the surface.

Bathsheba appears to be such a person, a woman as enigmatic as she is beautiful, as puzzling as she is powerful. Our introduction to Bathsheba (2 Sam 11) emphasized her attractiveness but told us nothing of her emotions. Was she thrilled or chilled by David's advances? We don't know. She came to David when called and coupled with him despite being married to another man, but we wonder if she had any choice.

Bathsheba's state of mind appears clearer when her infant son succumbs following a weeklong illness (2 Sam 12). That story is almost entirely devoted to David, however. We may assume that she grieved the child's death, and the text speaks of David's efforts to "console his wife," but readers are left to fill in the emotional blanks as we imagine the feelings of a bereaved mother and wonder to what extent she appreciated David's comfort.

Our third encounter with Bathsheba (1 Kgs 1) leaves us still wondering about her relationship with David, with whom she no longer sleeps and before whom she bows. There is little question, however, about Bathsheba's allegiance to Solomon, the son born after David's efforts at consoling the loss of their first child. She willingly conspires with Nathan to pressure David into designating Solomon as the next king, favoring him over his older brother Adonijah.

Bathsheba's final episode in the biblical narrative is also fraught with ambiguity, leaving the reader to puzzle over the inner workings of the queen mother's mysterious mind.

A Bit of Background (2:1-12)

To understand the implications of the story, we must recognize that it is set in the early days of Solomon's reign, as the young king sought to establish himself. The narrator describes a deathbed conversation in which David imparts final words of advice and instruction to the new king (2:1-9). The speech consists of two parts that are so jarringly disparate that one suspects it has been embellished by an editorial hand.

The first part of David's dying directive reflects the traditional theology of Deuteronomy that pervades the books of Joshua, Judges, Samuel, and Kings so thoroughly that scholars refer to these books as the "Deuteronomistic History."

With clear references to the teachings of Deuteronomy and the divine promise of 2 Samuel 7, David admonished Solomon to be faithful and follow the teaching of the Torah, promising success if he would remain obedient to God.

The piety of verses 1-4 offers a sharp disconnect to verses 5-9, in which David instructs Solomon to settle some old accounts for him. Evidently, David never forgot—or forgave—a slight. David instructed Solomon to eliminate crusty Joab, who had served David faithfully at times but also undercut him more than once. Solomon was told to honor Barzillai and his sons, who had shown David kindness, but to take vengeance on Shimei, who had rained curses and rocks on David when he fled before Absalom (2 Sam 19:23).

Following David's death, the text says Solomon "sat on the throne of his father David; and his kingdom was firmly established" (v. 12). Not so firmly established, however, that it was not subject to threats. His rival, Adonijah, still lived.

Adonijah's Appeal (2:13-18)

As Solomon ascended to the throne, Bathsheba became the nation's first "queen mother" in residence, a position of high respect. When the historians who compiled 2 Kings collated their accounting of the kings of Israel and Judah, they often included the name of the queen mother, adding the name of her father and their home city when it was known (for example, see 2 Kgs 21:19; 22:1; 23:31, 36; 24:8, 18).

As queen mother, Bathsheba may have had some supervisory control over the king's harem, and presumably retained some influence with her son, the king. Thus, when Adonijah sought to obtain David's former concubine Abishag for himself, he first came to Bathsheba.

The reader is left to wonder why Adonijah would embark on such a patently suicidal enterprise. Our contemporary culture has little sympathy for the concept of a king who maintains a collection of both wives and concubines, but in the ancient world, the size of a king's harem (and his ability to sire children by them) was a sign of his virility and power.

Indeed, the increasing power of kingship in Israel could be illustrated by the number of women at the king's disposal. In addition to at least one wife, Saul had only one concubine who is named (2 Sam 3:7), while David had multiple wives and at least ten concubines, for he left that many to mind the palace when he fled during Absalom's revolt (2 Sam 3:2-5, 13-16; 5:13-16; 15:16; 20:3). As Solomon expanded David's kingdom, it was said that he amassed 700 wives and 300 concubines (1 Kgs 11:3). The kingdom divided and shrank after Solomon, however. His son Rehoboam is said to have had eighteen wives (of whom he loved Maacah the daughter of Absalom most) and sixty concubines (2 Chr 11:21).

One sign of a new king's authority was his ability to possess his predecessor's concubines. Consequently, any rival's desire to take one of the former king's concubines was regarded as a power grab that could lead to insurrection. Thus, Saul's son Ishbaal (also called Ishbosheth) split with his powerful general Abner after accusing him of sleeping with Saul's former concubine, Rizpah (2 Sam 3:6-8). And, when the usurping Absalom and his troops swept into Jerusalem, Absalom proclaimed his new power by forcing the ten concubines David had left to the roof of the palace, where he engaged them in public sex for political effect, an act that Nathan had foreseen (2 Sam 12:8; 16:20-22).

These stories were well known, and the custom was written large in royal circles. Why, then, would Adonijah have the *chutzpah* to ask for Abishag? Did he have a death wish? Did he harbor misguided hopes that possessing Abishag might provide the legitimacy he needed to mount another campaign for the throne? Had he learned that Abishag was present when Nathan and Bathsheba convinced David to name Solomon king, and made plans to use her in undermining Solomon's kingdom? Was he simply so full of himself that he was blind to the repercussions of his daring request, thinking Absalom would grant him Abishag as a consolation prize?

We cannot nail down Adonijah's motives any more than we can state with certainty why Bathsheba agreed to intercede for him with Solomon. Did Bathsheba feel sorry for him? Did she see his request as an opportune way to get the presence of her dead husband's gorgeous bedmate out of the house? Or is it more likely that she knew Solomon would never grant Adonijah's request, and shrewdly pretended to be on his side while knowing that Solomon's response would be deadly? In 1 Kings 1, Bathsheba expressed fear that she and Solomon would be in imminent danger if Adonijah's bid for the throne were successful. Does she now perceive a perfect opportunity to terminate the same man who might have eliminated her?

Adonijah's visit to Bathsheba highlights the pretender's trepidation. He knew he was on shaky ground when she greeted him with a cold question: "Do you come in peace?" "*Shalom*," the word she used, can indicate peace, but also wholeness or integrity.

In typically Hebrew fashion, Adonijah answered with a single word: "*Shalom*." He then stumbled over himself, finding it difficult to get to the point: "A word I [want to] have with you."

Now it was Bathsheba's turn to respond with a single word: "Speak." The Hebrew verb for "speak" is pronounced differently but spelled the same as the noun that means "word," or "something." The narrator, then, has Bathsheba respond to Adonijah's request to say something by using the same term to say "speak," or as the NRSV puts it, "Go on."

Adonijah blurts out words that seem to betray his heart, asserting that Bathsheba knows the kingdom was once his and "all Israel" wanted him to be king before circumstances changed and Yahweh's activity made it "my brother's" (v. 15). The statement suggests that Adonijah had lost touch with reality, at least from the narrator's point of view: his earlier attempt at self-enthronement was never legitimate, and the only popular acclaim related in 1 Kings 1 was for Solomon, not him.

Having revealed more than he intended, perhaps, Adonijah hesitates again, as if afraid to come to the point. He indicates just one request and pleads with Bathsheba not to refuse (v. 16), eliciting another one-word reply from the queen mother: "Speak."

Finally, Adonijah states his purpose, asking Bathsheba to request that Solomon give Abishag to him (v. 17). Adonijah's assertion that "he will not refuse you" attests to the influence Bathsheba was known to have, but also to the huge miscalculation Adonijah had made.

Bathsheba's response is a bit cryptic. "Good," she said, and with an emphatic use of the personal pronoun, "I will speak to the king for [or about] you" (v. 18). The preposition Bathsheba used could mean "on your behalf," but it could also mean "concerning." Was Bathsheba planning to intercede, or to tattle?

Bathsheba's Request (2:19-21)

The queen mother's interview with Solomon illustrates the respect and even deference the young king showed to his mother: "The king rose to meet her, and bowed down to her; then he sat on his throne, and had a throne brought for the king's mother, and she sat on his right" (v. 19b).

Solomon's bowing before his mother and insistence that she sit on a throne at his right (indicative of favor/power) suggests that she had become a force in the court. It also implies that the audience was a public affair rather than a private conversation.

Bathsheba's brief speech gives the impression that she looked with favor on Adonijah's request and spoke in his behalf. Tweaking his words slightly, she asked "one *small* request" and added "do not refuse me" (v. 20a). Solomon's response was wholly positive: "Make your request, my mother; for I will not refuse you" (v. 20b).

Solomon's Response (2:22-25)

When Solomon learns what Bathsheba was asking, however—"Let Abishag the Shunammite be given to your brother Adonijah as his wife"—his promise of non-refusal is quickly forgotten. He immediately recognized the political implications of Adonijah's request and assumed that his former conspiracy to gain the throne remained alive: "And why do you ask Abishag the Shunammite for Adonijah? Ask for him the kingdom as well! For he is my elder brother; ask not only for him but also for the priest Abiathar and for Joab son of Zeruiah!" (v. 22).

On the surface of the story, Solomon appears to be rebuking his mother's effrontery, but what the reader does not know is whether both he and Bathsheba were winking as they spoke. When Solomon swore a double oath that Adonijah would be put to death, the outcome may have been exactly as Bathsheba had planned.

Notes

Notes

nextsunday
STUDIES

1 Peter
Keep Hope Alive

This study of First Peter focuses on keeping hope alive in the face of pressures and circumstances that could possibly extinguish it completely, or worse, turn authentic faith into a pale replica of the real thing.

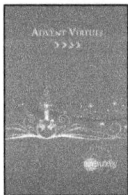

Advent Virtues

The phrase "holiday rush" is not an exaggeration. The frantic pace required to purchase gifts, bake holiday foods, and attend Christmas parties, plays, and performances takes its toll; we arrive at Christmas Day exhausted. Within the context of December busyness, the ancient Christian season of Advent takes on new meaning and acquires renewed importance. May God instill the virtues of *hope, peace, joy, love,* and *faith* in each of us this Advent.

Apocalyptic Literature

This study examines five apocalyptic texts in the Bible—from Zechariah, Daniel, Matthew, and Revelation. With each new year bringing a new prediction of impending doom, it is always a perfect time to get the story straight. Apocalyptic literature does not address the future. It addresses our present.

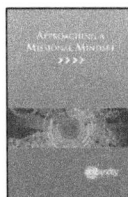

Approaching a Missional Mindset

The World isn't the same as it once was. We must be the church in a new place, in unimagined ways, and with a wider range of people. Engage your small group with the radical and refreshing challenge of developing a "missional lifestyle."

Baptist Freedom
Celebrating Our Baptist Heritage
What makes a Baptist a Baptist? Of course, the ultimate answer is simple: membership in a local Baptist church. But there are all kinds of Baptist churches! What are the spiritual and theological marks of a Baptist? What is the shape and the feel of Baptist Christianity?

The Bible and the Arts
God has used artistic expression throughout the centuries to convey truth, offer blessing, and urge believers to deeper faithfulness. In modern life, artistic expression flourishes, from movies to books to music to paintings to photographs. Sometimes artists are intentional about trying to portray God's truths. Other times, perhaps God is working even when the artist is unaware of it. As believers, we may hear and see God at work in many art forms.

The Birthday of a King
The first four lessons in this unit draw inspiration from a traditional interpretation of the Advent candles as the Prophets' Candle, the Bethlehem Candle, the Shepherds' Candle, and the Angels' Candle. The final lesson, which occurs after Advent, celebrates the theological meaning of Jesus' birth as described in the prologue to John's Gospel.

Challenges of the Christian Life
The way of the cross is difficult, and taking Jesus seriously means looking honestly at how we fall short of God's best hopes for us and seeing how much we need God's grace. For all of us there are times when we need to remember that Christ is our saving grace and recommit ourselves to the journey of faith, rediscovering, again and again, the life-giving purpose described in the book of Ephesians.

Christ Is Born!
Even in the midst of difficult circumstances, Advent is a time when we can find hope. Much like today, people in the 1st century church faced struggles. Examining the Gospel of Matthew, lessons include "Waiting for Christ," "Preparing for Christ," "Expecting Christ," "Announcing Christ," and "The Arrival of Christ."

Christians and Hunger

These sessions challenge us to apply gospel lenses and holy imagination to what literally gives us energy to live: food. With God's grace, we have the opportunity to imagine communities where tables are large and all are fed.

Christians and the Public Square

Politics and faith are tricky areas for Christians to negotiate. The First Amendment to the Constitution guarantees religious freedom for all Americans. As Christians who are also citizens, questions abound: How do we distinguish between faithful and unfaithful forms of civic engagement? How do we give Caesar his due while giving our all to God?

Christmas in Mark

In the early chapters of Mark, we will encounter a Christmas story. This story, however, will not be quite like the one told by other Gospel writers, but it will resonate with the reality of your life. Mark doesn't deny the beauty or reality of the nativity; however, he seems to believe that Christmas begins—the gospel begins—when Christ intrudes upon the hard realities of life.

The Church on a Mission

What does it mean to be a church on a mission? The lesson of Acts 1:8 is that we must simultaneously carry out Christ's mandate at home, in our region, in places that have been our blind spots, and around the world.

Colossians
Living the Faith Faithfully

Paul's letter to the Colossians begins with a high-minded philosophical defense of the faith, but concludes with a collection of extremely practical advice for living by faith. This study addresses the questions many Christians face today, helping them apply Paul's practical advice in their own lives.

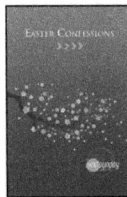

Easter Confessions

Easter confession is often found on many different lips in the Gospel of John. When we listen carefully, those ancient confessions still echo into this new millennium.

Embracing the Word of God

We live during a time of transition in Christian history. Basic assumptions about the truth of the Christian faith are being questioned, not only by nonbelievers, but by Christians themselves. First John offers a starting point for understanding of what it means to "be" Christian.

Esther: A Woman of Discretion and Valor

The book of Esther is not a record of historical facts as such. Rather, it is a magnificent narrative that refuses to interpret life as being driven by coincidence or happenstance. In the otherwise unknown characters of Esther, Haman, and Mordecai, we trace the movement of the divine hand as God collaborates with God's risk-taking people to rescue them from the hand of their enemies.

Facing Life's Challenges

This study explores four significant challenges common to most persons of faith: the challenge of new light, the challenge of time's limit, the challenge of living with mystery, and the challenge of authentic spirituality. Although these issues are neither simple nor easy to ponder, this study effectively leads us in confronting these challenges.

Forgiveness and Reconciliation

Forgiveness is a central issue in our capacity to remain redemptively connected to those relationships we prize. Restoring broken or interrupted relationships is a primary issue for all of us, and managing forgiveness is crucial to the possibility of experiencing reconciliation. Several dimensions of forgiveness affect our lives in significant ways. In this study, we attempt to address a few of those important issues.

The Four Cardinal Virtues

Christians are learning how to distinguish between members of a church and disciples of Christ. Discipleship involves developing virtues in those who come to our churches seeking life, salvation, grace, mercy. If we want to have something to offer a world in desperate need, then we must return to virtues like discernment, justice, courage, and moderation. We must return to the hard and glorious work of making disciples.

Godly Leadership

Nehemiah was called to return to Jerusalem to lead in the sacred task of rebuilding the city's walls. Displaying characteristics often lacking in secular leadership—prayerful humility, a willingness to work with diverse teams, wisdom in confronting conflict, and a passion to stand with the powerless—Nehemiah offered his people a portrait of godly leadership that can still shape our own calls to lead nearly 2,500 years later.

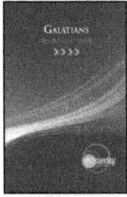

Galatians
Freedom in Christ

Paul wrote with fiery passion, as you will notice from the opening paragraphs of this letter to the Galatians. But his language reveals that he was writing about a crucially important issue—the very nature of salvation in Christ.

A Holy and Surprising Birth

Christmas begins here—discover these five love stories from the book of Luke and renew your appreciation of God's laborious effort to birth our salvation.

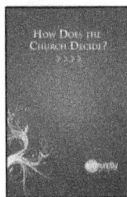

How Does the Church Decide?

An array of decisions draw energy and time from church members. These decisions may be theological, such as mode of baptism, aesthetic, such as the color of the sanctuary carpet, or functional, such as the selection of a new minister. This study will consider how the church has made its decisions in the past to help guide our decisions today.

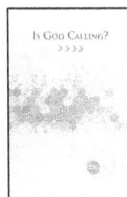

Is God Calling?

Witness the varying forms of God's call, the variety of people called, and the variety of responses. Perhaps God's call to you will become clearer.

James
Gaining True Wisdom
If we'll be honest with God and ourselves as we study what James says, we can make great strides toward wisdom and a living faith.

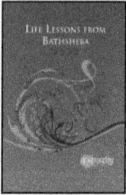

Life Lessons from Bathsheba
Who was Bathsheba? She was a complex figure who developed from the silent object of David's lust into a powerful, vocal, and influential queen mother.

Life Lessons from David
In the Bible, we catch David in the various stages of the human journey: childhood, adolescence, adulthood, and senior adulthood. From the biblical treatment of the stages of David's life, we can land some insights to assist us in better understanding the human journey.

The Matriarchs
The matriarchs of Genesis offer their lives as a testimony of faith, perseverance, and audacity. We learn from their mistakes and suffering. We will gain the hope of Hagar, the joy of Sarah, and the audacity of Rebekah as we are challenged to examine our prejudices and our insecurities while studying Esau and Jacob's wives.

Missional Hospitality
If we are serious about following Jesus, we will be people of open hearts, open hands, and open homes. In other words, as followers of Jesus we will practice the fine art of hospitality. In lesson one, we reflect on hospitality to strangers. In lesson two, we address hospitality to the poor. In lesson three, we focus on hospitality to sinners. In lesson four, we learn about hospitality to newcomers. Lesson five reminds us about our hospitality to Christ.

Moses
From the Burning Bush to the Promised Land
We would do well to trace the life of Moses so we might discover how his life changed, both personally and as Israel's leader, as he learned what it meant to love God with all his heart, soul, and strength.

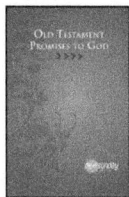

Old Testament Promises to God

Some individuals may feel that our promises couldn't possibly mean anything to God. Perhaps the real question is this: under what circumstances should or do we make such promises? The Old Testament contains several examples of people making promises to God, using the unique form of a biblical "vow."

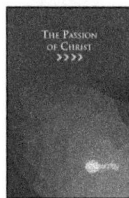

The Passion of Christ

The four lessons in this unit highlight the faith struggles of the early disciples. In lesson one, Jesus addresses the issues of faith and practice. In lesson two, we meet Judas who, like us, struggled with God's Kingdom and human kingdoms. In lesson three, the issue of temptation reminds us that our faith journey is a constant challenge. Lesson Four invites us to remember Peter's experience of "faith failure." Peter's failure, however, is not the final word. There is forgiveness.

The Prayer Life of Jesus

The study of Jesus' prayer life can deepen our own prayer practices. These five sessions examine the importance of prayer at various stages of Jesus' life and ministry. He made no important decisions without consulting God.

Prepare the Way

In these sessions, we will seek to prepare the way toward and into the Christmas season. We begin with the theme of hopeful watchfulness in light of the coming of Christ. Next, we will spend two sessions considering the ministry of John the Baptist, the forerunner of Christ. Then, we will consider Matthew's account of the birth of Jesus and join in wonder at the miracle of "God with us." Finally, we will remember the story of the "holy innocents" killed by Herod in his attempt to eliminate the Christ child's threat to his power.

Proverbs for Living

Long ago, a collection of wise teachers committed themselves to the ways of God and collected this wisdom into what we know as the book of Proverbs. These four lessons explore the simple truth of Proverbs: there is a good life to be had—a life lived in faithfulness to God.

Qualities of Our Missional God

Too often we are tempted to let "numbers" drive missions. The book of Numbers reminds us that missions is motivated by something deeper. Missions reflects the heart and nature of God. If we can just get past the math, we can see God's nature clearly in the book of Numbers. . . in the wilderness.

Responding to the Resurrection

All major events of human history elicit responses as varied as the personalities and situations represented by those affected. No one witnesses a world-changing event without being affected in some way. Studying the response of early followers helps us to shape our own response to the resurrection of Jesus. Each of us must consider our response to Jesus' life, teachings, death, resurrection, and call on our lives.

The Seven Deadly Sins

What exactly is sin? Just as we organize our cupboards and our schedules to make sense of our lives, Christian thinkers have organized sin into a number of categories in order to understand and surrender these patterns to God. The notion of "seven deadly sins" emerged as a way to recognize specific dangers to our spiritual lives. The purpose of the book is to guide people away from sin and into a wise and godly life.

Seeking Holiness in the Sermon on the Mount

The Sermon on the Mount has long been recognized as the pinnacle of Jesus' teaching. But with this importance in mind, it's easy to think of Jesus' teachings as lofty and idealistic, offering little guidance for everyday life. Perhaps Jesus' sermon allows us to see beyond ourselves, beyond our own failures and shortcomings—revealing God's intention for our lives.

Spiritual Disciplines
Obligation or Opportunity?

The spiritual disciplines help deepen a believer's faith and increases his or her intimacy with Christ. In this study, we take a deeper look at some of the disciplines and consider their practice as a response to God's love.

Sing We Now of Christmas

In this study, we will explore some familiar prophecies, as well as the Gospel birth narratives, through the lens of five traditional Christmas carols. As carols have grown to be a fuller and more meaningful part of our worship and celebration, so too can the stories of Jesus' birth continue to grow within us and enrich our faith experience.

Stewardship
A Way of Living

Great News! Stewardship is not about money! At least not *just* about money. Certainly, stewardship relates to money, and, yes, we need to tithe. However, stewardship branches out into multiple areas of life. Properly practiced, this act of service can lead to peace and purpose in living.

The Ten Commandments

When the Ten Commandments are in the news, it is usually because a judge or teacher has hung them up on the walls. The Ten Commandments do not need to be posted or even preached nearly so much as they need to be practiced and viewed as life-giving, joyful affirmations of a better way of life.

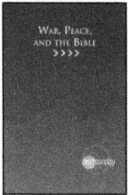

War, Peace, and the Bible

As people of faith, we are faced daily with an expectation that we participate in violent actions, our willingness to allow violence in the world to continue, and our response to violence in our lives. Is there a place for war and violence in our faith?

What Would Jesus Say?
A Lenten Study

To address what Jesus would say, we need to discover what Jesus did say. These lessons will attempt to help us understand Jesus' teachings and apply them today.

The Wonder of Easter

In 1 Corinthians 15, Paul asserts that the message that Jesus died for our sins, was buried, and rose on the third day is "of first importance" (v. 3). It is the core of the gospel story and of the Christian faith. But as much as Easter is a mystery to contemplate, it is also a hope to embrace and good news to proclaim.

**NextSunday Studies
are available from**

NextSunday
Resources

www.ingramcontent.com/pod-product-compliance
Lightning Source LLC
Chambersburg PA
CBHW060652030426
42337CB00017B/2574